W9-BJR-309

## DATE DUE

| | | | |
|---|---|---|---|
| | | | |
| | | | |
| | | | |
| | | | |
| | | | |
| | | | |
| | | | |
| | | | |
| | | | |
| | | | |
| | | | |
| | | | |

# Franklin D. ROOSEVELT

DAVID TAYLOR

Heinemann Library
Chicago, Illinois

Customer Service 888-454-2279

Visit our website at www.heinemannlibrary.com

Designed by AMR
Illustrated by Art Construction
Originated by Dot Gradations
Printed in China

05 04 03 02 01
10 9 8 7 6 5 4 3 2 1

**Library of Congress Cataloging-in-Publication Data**
Taylor, David, 1945 July 10-
    Franklin Delano Roosevelt / David Taylor.
        p. cm. -- (Leading lives)
    Includes bibliographical references (p.   ) and index.
    ISBN 1-58810-161-4
    1. Roosevelt, Franklin D. (Franklin Delano), 1882-1945--Juvenile
    literature. 2. Presidents--United States--Biography--Juvenile
    literature. [1. Roosevelt, Franklin D. (Franklin Delano), 1882-1945. 2.
    Presidents.] I. Title. II. Series.

E807 .T38 2001
973.917'092--dc21

                                                00-012839

**Acknowledgments**
The publishers would like to thank the following for permission to reproduce photographs:
AKG, p. 19; Associated Press, p. 35; Corbis, pp. 4, 15, 21, 23, 37, 39; Ethel Davies, p. 55; Franklin D. Roosevelt Library, pp. 5, 11, 14, 17, 20, 27, 28, 31, 32, 42, 46, 47, 51; Hulton Getty, pp. 8, 12, 24, 45; Imperial War Museum, p. 54; Popperfoto, pp. 6, 48.

Cover photograph reproduced with permission of Camera Press.

Our thanks to Christopher Gibb for his comments in the preparation of this book.

Every effort has been made to contact copyright holders of any material reproduced in this book. Any omissions will be rectified in subsequent printings if notice is given to the publishers.

Some words are shown in bold, **like this.** You can find out what they mean by looking in the glossary.

# Contents

# 1 Giver of Hope

In 1932, the American nation was in the depths of despair. The country was suffering the worst economic crisis in its history. Millions were out of work, and desperate people roamed the streets looking for work and a bite to eat from a **soup kitchen.** Herbert Hoover, the **Republican** president, appeared to be doing little to help the situation. One American complained, "I am afraid. Every man is afraid."

FOR A SUMMARY OF THE U.S. SYSTEM OF GOVERNMENT, SEE PAGE 59.

It was no surprise when Hoover was voted out of office in November 1932. The new president was Franklin Delano Roosevelt, a **Democrat** from the state of New York. The American people identified with his cheerful optimism and saw him as a symbol of hope. They were certain he was the right person to put the country back on its feet, and they were further reassured by his "fireside chats," a series of radio talks in which he spoke calmly to the nation.

A second crisis was to confront Roosevelt. In 1939, World War II broke out in Europe. To begin with, the U.S. was not directly involved in the fighting but, after the Japanese attacked **Pearl Harbor** in 1941, the country declared war. Roosevelt now had the monumental task of guiding the U.S. through the conflict.

▲ Franklin Roosevelt is pictured giving one of his famous radio "fireside chats" in 1933.

▶ *Here, President Roosevelt reviews American troops in North Africa in 1943.*

The American people felt that there was "an experienced hand on the tiller" and, even in the darkest days of the war, were confident that Roosevelt would lead them to victory.

Roosevelt's cheerful image, however, hid a personal tragedy. An attack of **polio** in 1921 had left him paralyzed from the waist down. Yet he fought back to become the only person to be elected president on four occasions. In 1983, 38 years after his death, a group of noted historians voted Roosevelt the second greatest American president of all time. Only Abraham Lincoln, who was president from 1861 to 1865 and is credited with the abolition of slavery, was ranked higher. So who was Franklin Roosevelt, how did he rise to the presidency, and what was his impact on U.S. and world history?

## Roosevelt's gift
*"Hope was in fact Franklin Roosevelt's greatest gift to his fellow Americans . . . He gave us hope because all could see that he himself felt not the slightest doubt about the future at any time in his years as president."*

(Joseph Alsop, an American political journalist, speaking in 1982)

# 2 A Gentlemanly Upbringing

In 1867, James Roosevelt, a successful businessman whose ancestors had migrated to the United States from Holland in the 1640s, purchased the country estate of Springwood in New York state. The Springwood estate was situated among gentle hills and woodlands near the village of Hyde Park, some 85 miles (135 kilometers) north of the city of New York. James Roosevelt (1828–1900) was a pillar of the Hyde Park community, serving on the school board and as churchwarden. He was also wealthy enough to spend a lot of his time at leisure, holding frequent dinner parties at his seventeen-room mansion.

In 1880, at the age of 52, James, a widower, married his distant cousin Sara Delano Roosevelt, who was just half his age. On

January 30, 1882, Sara gave birth to her only child, a boy named Franklin Delano. Young Franklin had a happy but isolated upbringing. He was educated at home, first by a **governess** and then by a private tutor who taught him math, science, French, Latin, history, and geography. He was not allowed to mix with the local Hyde Park children, as his parents

◀ *This is Franklin, at age eleven, with his mother, Sara. She was to have a considerable influence on his life.*

considered them to be unsuitable companions for their son. Franklin loved the countryside and had numerous pastimes, including horse-riding, collecting birds' eggs, photography, and stamp collecting.

Sara and James Roosevelt adored Franklin. They taught him to have excellent manners and expected him to respect other people. In other ways, however, they stifled him. He was not allowed to wear long pants until he was eight, which was older than usual, and Sara organized every moment of his day.

The Roosevelt family traveled widely in the U.S. and made frequent visits to Europe. By the age of fifteen, Franklin had crossed the Atlantic Ocean eight times. Every summer the family took a vacation at their cottage on **Campobello Island,** New Brunswick. It was here that Franklin developed a passion for the sea and became an expert yachtsman.

## The Groton years, 1896–1900

In 1896, Franklin, at age fourteen, was sent away to be educated at Groton Preparatory School in Massachusetts. Groton catered to students from privileged backgrounds, and its headmaster, the Reverend Endicott Peabody, believed that the school had a duty to train its students for public service. As a result, the rules were strict. The students slept in crudely furnished dormitories and were expected to be polite, organized, and punctual. Among the subjects studied were Latin, Greek, German, French, mathematics, and science. Franklin's academic record at Groton was above average, and Peabody regarded him as an "intelligent and faithful scholar."

Initially, Franklin found it difficult to make friends. The other students had already been at Groton for two years when he arrived, and they looked upon him with suspicion.

To compensate, Franklin tried to gain acceptance by joining as many sports teams as possible, but he was only good enough to make the second team in hockey, football, and baseball.

Outside speakers frequently visited Groton to talk to the students about the lives of the poor and underprivileged. These talks made an impression on Franklin, and he was inspired to help out at a summer camp run by the school for poor youngsters from New York and Boston. In 1897, Peabody invited Franklin's cousin, Theodore Roosevelt, to visit Groton. Theodore was making his way in politics and, at the time, was the assistant secretary to the United States Navy. Franklin was captivated by his cousin and came to regard him as a role model. By 1900, Franklin was more popular with his fellow students and enjoyed a reputation as the school's best public debater. His four years at Groton played a crucial role in shaping his character and attitude toward life.

◀ *Groton School's second football team is shown here. Franklin Roosevelt is in the middle of the front row.*

## Theodore Roosevelt

Theodore "Teddy" Roosevelt (1858–1919) came from a wealthy New York family. In 1897, he was made assistant secretary to the United States Navy. He fought in Cuba during the Spanish-American War of 1898 and became a national hero when he led a courageous cavalry charge during the battle for San Juan. Following this, he was elected the **Republican** governor of New York state and, in 1900, he became the vice president of the United States. He took over as president when William McKinley was assassinated in 1901, and remained in office until 1909. As president, Theodore Roosevelt advocated the reforms of the **Progressive era** and believed that it was necessary for the **federal government** to play a part in managing industry and business. Franklin D. Roosevelt was later to adopt a similar philosophy.

FOR A SUMMARY OF THE U.S. SYSTEM OF GOVERNMENT, SEE PAGE 59.

## Harvard and marriage

In September 1900, Franklin enrolled at Harvard University in Massachusetts to study history and government. Shortly afterward, his father, James Roosevelt, died at the age of 72. Franklin was shocked and upset and returned home to comfort his mother, who soon moved to Boston to be near her son.

Franklin was so busy with his social life, attending parties and dances, that he found it difficult to concentrate fully on his studies at Harvard. He was eager to make his mark as a sportsman, but was not selected for either the football or rowing team.

Franklin received another setback when his application to join "Porcellian," the most famous Harvard social club, was turned down. He later said this was the "greatest disappointment" of his life. Instead, Franklin began working for the *Crimson*, the university's newspaper. He enhanced his reputation by writing articles on politics and sports and, in January 1903, became the paper's editor.

In 1902, Franklin started dating Anna Eleanor Roosevelt, a distant cousin. The couple announced their engagement in November 1903. Sara Roosevelt, Franklin's mother, was lukewarm about the relationship. She said they were too young to get married but, in truth, she most likely did not want another woman to come between her and Franklin. Nevertheless, Franklin and Eleanor were married in New York on March 17, 1905. The Reverend Endicott Peabody conducted the ceremony, and the bride was given away by her uncle, President Theodore Roosevelt. After honeymooning in Europe, the young couple rented a townhouse on East 36th Street in New York.

In 1906, their first child, Anna, was born, followed by James in 1907. By this time Franklin was studying law at Columbia Law School in New York, but his studies did not hold his interest. He passed the exam to practice law in 1907 and found a job as a junior clerk with a well-known New York law firm, but that too proved unsatisfactory. He found the work routine and dull, and hated being tied to a desk all day. Meanwhile, his mother financed the building of a new house on East 65th Street as a "Christmas present to Franklin and Eleanor." In 1908, she moved in to live with the family.

In 1909, Franklin Jr. was born, but he died from pneumonia at the age of seven months. Roosevelt now needed a fresh challenge to take his mind off the painful death of his third child and the boredom of his job. He frequently told his colleagues that he intended to follow his cousin, Theodore, into politics at the first opportunity. It was not to be long before the chance arrived.

◄ *Eleanor and Franklin Roosevelt posed for this photograph in the spring of 1905.*

# 3 Early Political Experiences

FOR A SUMMARY OF THE U.S. SYSTEM OF GOVERNMENT, SEE PAGE 59.

In 1910, the **Democratic** Party leaders in New York state asked Roosevelt to run for election to the state senate. He was nominated because he was from a well-known family and had enough private money to finance his campaign. Roosevelt eagerly accepted the invitation and faced the challenge with enthusiasm. Few people thought he would win, as the district he was contesting was a **Republican** stronghold. Renting a red Maxwell touring car, Roosevelt drove around meeting as many ordinary people as possible. His first speeches were nervously delivered, but gradually his confidence grew, and he won the election by over 1,000 votes. Another joyful event in 1910 was the birth of the Roosevelts' fourth child, Elliott.

Roosevelt was 28 years old when he moved his family into a large house in Albany, the capital of New York state, and took up his seat in the state senate. During the summers, when the senate was not in session, the family would spend time at their home on **Campobello Island.**

As a state senator, Roosevelt announced that he wanted to help farmers and fight for better working conditions. He also said that natural resources, such as woodlands, should be conserved.

◀ Roosevelt was photographed in 1911 when he was a New York state senator.

Some of the top men in the Democratic Party, however, became irritated when Roosevelt began to criticize the way the party was run. A leading New York Democrat, "Big Tim" Sullivan, called him an "awful, arrogant fellow."

## Further success in the political arena

In 1912, Roosevelt ran for a second term of office in the state senate. At the time, he was ill with typhoid fever and bedridden, so he employed Louis McHenry Howe, a newspaper reporter, to be his campaign agent. Howe did the job brilliantly, distributing posters, leaflets, and advertisements telling the voters that Roosevelt would support farmers and workers. Roosevelt was reelected with 62 percent of the vote, and Howe was to remain his adviser and confidant until his death in 1936. There was a great deal of media interest in Franklin's political career. Numerous newspaper articles highlighted the fact that he was following in the exact footsteps of his cousin, Theodore.

During the 1912 presidential election campaign, Roosevelt gave his wholehearted support to Woodrow Wilson (see page 58), the Democratic candidate. Wilson won the election and became the 28th president of the United States. In 1913, Wilson rewarded Roosevelt for his support, giving him the position of assistant secretary to the U.S. Navy, a post that had previously been occupied by Theodore. Roosevelt moved his family from New York into rented property in Washington, D.C., and tackled his new job with relish. When the U.S. entered **World War I** in April 1917, he organized the Navy to convey soldiers and weapons to Europe.

## Trouble in the family

There were two more additions to the Roosevelt family during this period, Franklin Jr. in 1914 and John in 1916.

Eleanor commented that between the years 1905 and 1917, she was "always getting over a baby or having one." Meanwhile, Roosevelt worked long hours and his children did not see very much of him. Eleanor had the full responsibility of looking after domestic affairs and disciplining the children.

Roosevelt and Eleanor began to grow apart. She was shy and felt awkward around people. On the other hand, her husband was outgoing and loved throwing parties for his Washington friends. Eleanor was also resentful of Sara Roosevelt, who was a dominant figure in the family. Eleanor and the children spent the summer months on **Campobello Island,** while Roosevelt was only able to join them for brief spells.

In late 1918, Eleanor discovered that Roosevelt was having a romantic affair with Lucy Mercer, a young woman who had worked as her social secretary. Eleanor was deeply hurt. The couple patched up their differences, but the affair left a long-lasting scar on their marriage.

◀ The Roosevelt family is shown here on vacation at Campobello Island. Franklin, Sara, and Eleanor are sitting at the back. The five children in the front are, from left to right, Elliott, Franklin Jr., John, Anna, and James.

▶ *This is the front of a Democratic Party song sheet from the 1920 election. The U.S. was destined never to become a member of the League of Nations.*

## The 1920 presidential election

In 1920, James M. Cox of Ohio, the **Democratic** candidate for the presidency, asked Roosevelt to run as his vice president. Cox believed that the fame of the Roosevelt name would help him win. Roosevelt, now 38 years old, was highly flattered and campaigned tirelessly. Accompanied by Eleanor, he visited 32 states and made over 1,000 speeches. Cox and Roosevelt argued that the U.S. should play a full role in international affairs and join the **League of Nations,** a newly formed international body, to keep the peace and settle disputes between countries. It was a message that fell mainly on deaf ears. Many Americans wanted their country to keep out of world affairs. The Republican candidate, Warren G. Harding, favored **isolationism** and won a landslide victory to become the new president. Roosevelt was disappointed but not disheartened. He had met people from all walks of life and become a national personality. The campaign had turned him into an excellent public speaker, skilled at building an excellent relationship with his audience. He was thus well equipped for future election campaigns.

After the presidential election campaign of 1920, Roosevelt returned to work in New York, where he established the law firm of Emmet, Marvin, and Roosevelt. He kept in touch with politics, making sure he knew what was happening within the **Democratic** Party. In the summer of 1921, the Roosevelt family went to their home on **Campobello Island** for a well-earned rest. Franklin was exhausted. He had not had a vacation for three years and needed to recharge his batteries.

## Polio strikes

One day in August, Roosevelt, at age 39, and two of his sons went swimming in an ice-cold lagoon and then jogged home in their wet bathing suits. In the evening, Roosevelt felt unwell and retired early to bed. When he woke up he had a fever, his left leg had gone numb, and he had difficulty getting out of bed. He then developed severe pains in his neck and back. A local doctor was called, and he said Roosevelt was suffering from a heavy chill. Roosevelt was in great pain, and a second doctor recommended massage and rest. In the end, a specialist summoned from Boston diagnosed **polio,** a viral infection of the nervous system. The disease left Roosevelt paralyzed from the waist down, and he soon had to face the fact that he would never walk again.

Over the next few months Roosevelt gradually learned to live with his disability. Heavy steel braces were fitted to his legs and, with the aid of crutches, he learned to walk a few steps. The braces enabled him to make speeches standing up, and he built up his upper body so he was able to hoist himself into a wheelchair. He kept a cheerful disposition to cover up his disability, and said that he did not want anyone to feel sorry for him—even telling one newspaper reporter that he did not "want any sob stuff."

## Warm Springs, Georgia

In 1924, Roosevelt visited Warm Springs, a run-down health spa in the state of Georgia. He found that he benefited greatly from bathing in the swimming pool, which contained naturally warm mineral water. Roosevelt was so impressed that he spent $200,000 rebuilding the resort, turning it into a major treatment center for polio sufferers worldwide. He was to visit Warm Springs regularly throughout the rest of his life.

▶ A smiling Franklin Roosevelt managed to stand upright with the help of his servant and his doctor in 1925.

# The Road to the Presidency

Roosevelt did not return to politics until 1924, when he made a speech at the **Democratic** Party **Convention** at Madison Square Garden in New York. The delegates gave him a rousing reception as he struggled to reach the podium on his crutches.

## The prosperous twenties

For most Americans, the 1920s were years of prosperity. People were able to pay for goods such as motor cars, radios, and refrigerators, all by monthly installments. Unemployment was low and living standards were high. Many people made money by buying and selling **shares** at a profit on the **stock market.** The **Republicans,** who were in power throughout the 1920s, took the credit for this prosperity. They said that it resulted from the fact that the government did not interfere in the world of business and industry.

In 1928, Roosevelt was asked to run for governor of New York state. His first reaction was to turn down the invitation. He wanted to continue his treatment at Warm Springs and, besides, the Democratic Party was in disarray. Eventually, he was persuaded to run and, as usual, fought a brilliant campaign. Against all the odds, Roosevelt narrowly won the contest and was installed as governor of New York state on January 1, 1929.

Roosevelt worked hard as governor. One of his advisers said that "his disability had no effect upon his energy." Roosevelt gave financial help to farmers and asked the state senate to spend more on hospitals, parks, and schools. Family life was also hectic during this period. During the school vacations the Roosevelt house in Albany was always a hive of activity, as the four boys would bring their school friends to stay. By now, Eleanor had become far more confident and regularly invited influential local people to dinner.

## The Wall Street crash

In October 1929, the Wall Street Stock Exchange in New York crashed when share prices fell very sharply. Overnight, shares became worthless. People who had paid high prices for shares in the early 1920s lost all their money. People stopped investing money in industry and businesses, many of which were forced to close down. Soon the entire United States was gripped by the **Great Depression.** Unemployment soared and millions were thrown into poverty.

By 1931, the Depression had left 8 million Americans out of work, including 1 million in the state of New York alone. There was no social security in the U.S. at this time, and unemployed people relied on charities for help. **Soup kitchens** were set up and people searched garbage cans for scraps of food. Roosevelt decided to act. In August 1931, he set up the Temporary Emergency Relief Administration (TERA) in New York state. This was a state-funded agency that provided food, clothing, and shelter to those in need and helped the jobless find work.

▶ *Roosevelt, as governor of New York, found time for a chat with a member of the public at Hyde Park station in November 1930.*

To finance the agency, Roosevelt increased taxes and gained $20 million. It was the first time in American history that a state government had intervened directly to combat unemployment and poverty.

## Roosevelt runs for president

In July 1932, Roosevelt won the **Democratic** Party's nomination to run against Herbert Hoover in the upcoming presidential election. In accepting the nomination in Chicago, Roosevelt told the audience: "I pledge you, I pledge myself, to a new deal for the American people." In the election campaign that followed, Roosevelt toured the U.S. in the "Roosevelt Special," a specially chartered train. Wherever the train stopped, Roosevelt spoke to the local people from the platform of the rear carriage, telling them that it was the job of the government to tackle the Depression. People liked his optimism and his enthusiasm. Here was a man who gave them hope for the future. By now, unemployment had reached 12 million (24 percent of the working population), and President Hoover had become very unpopular for not doing enough to help those who were out of work. In November, Roosevelt easily won the presidential election, receiving 57 percent of the popular vote and winning 42 of the 48 states.

◀ *This is a Democratic campaign badge from 1932.*

## Herbert Hoover

Hoover was born in West Branch, Iowa. He started life as a businessman and mining engineer, before turning to politics in the early 1900s. Hoover joined the Republican Party and became president of the U.S. in 1928. He did little to tackle the Depression, saying it was not the job of the **federal government** to provide money and food for the unemployed. Unlike Roosevelt, Hoover came across as a pessimist who hardly ever smiled. A popular saying of the time was: "In Hoover we trusted and now we are busted."

▲ Temporary shelters were built by the homeless in Central Park in New York City. People mockingly nicknamed these shelters "Hoovervilles" after the unpopular President Herbert Hoover.

At that time, newly elected presidents had to wait four months before taking office. As Roosevelt awaited his inauguration, the **Great Depression** deepened. Factories were closed and farmers were forced to destroy crops they were unable to sell. People felt helpless and there was a mood of desperation. The president-elect, however, was not idle. He was busy discussing ways of fighting the Depression with a team of expert advisers.

On March 4, 1933, **Inauguration Day,** Roosevelt took the oath of office and then turned to address a crowd of 100,000 in front of the Capitol building in Washington, DC. In a forthright speech he said that "the only thing we have to fear is fear itself," and he promised Americans "action and action now." It was an inspiring address. The American people were hopeful that Roosevelt would solve the country's problems.

## Reaching the people

Roosevelt's first task was to tackle the banking crisis. People had lost confidence in the banks and had been withdrawing their savings. Much of the money deposited in banks is loaned out in **mortgages** or invested. As a result, many banks did not have the hard currency readily available to meet the demand and were forced to close their doors. On March 9, under powers given to him by the Emergency Banking Act, Roosevelt closed down every bank in the country and sent out agents to inspect their books. Only those banks that were financially sound were allowed to reopen. On March 12, Roosevelt explained what he had done to 60 million radio listeners. In the first of his "fireside chats," he used straightforward language to appeal to as wide an audience as possible. His mellow voice was easy to listen to, and the next day people responded to the president's talk by putting their money back into the banks that had been shown to be financially sound.

Roosevelt wanted to cultivate a good relationship with the press, so he started holding open press conferences. Journalists were allowed into the White House to question him. No longer would they be required to submit written questions. Instead they were free to ask the president questions "off the cuff." In return, they were requested not to take photographs showing the president's disability or ask questions about it. The request was fully respected and, interestingly, the many newspaper cartoons drawn of Roosevelt always depict him as a person who had full use of his legs. This shows the respect journalists had for Roosevelt.

▲ The first open press conference was held in the White House on March 8, 1933. These conferences were entertaining and very popular with journalists.

## Alphabet agencies

On March 9, 1933, **Congress** was summoned into session. With 12 million Americans out of work, Roosevelt knew that the **federal government** had to create jobs to "get the wheels of the economy turning again." Roosevelt argued that if people had jobs, they would have money to spend. This would create a demand for goods and factories would reopen. Over a period of 100 days up to June 16, a series of New Deal agencies—nicknamed "alphabet agencies" because they were known by their initials—were set up.

Roosevelt knew that the jobless had to be helped. The Federal Emergency Relief Agency (FERA) gave $500 million of federal money to states to help feed and clothe the unemployed. Other alphabet agencies were set up to create jobs, including the Civilian Conservation Corps (CCC) and the Public Works Administration (PWA). The CCC employed young men, ages 18–25, to do conservation work, such as planting trees and strengthening riverbanks to stop flooding. They were paid a small wage plus food, clothing, and shelter. The PWA employed the jobless to build houses, roads, bridges, and hospitals across the U.S.

◀ This political cartoon shows Roosevelt, now nicknamed FDR, and Congress handing out "alphabet agency medicine" to a sick U.S.

Next, Roosevelt tried to regulate businesses by setting up the National Recovery Administration (NRA). The NRA encouraged businesses to set up codes of good practice, which involved charging fair prices and paying workers a decent wage. Businesses that joined the plan displayed a "blue eagle" motif on their products. The first New Deal also tried to help the farming community. Too much food was being grown, and this meant farmers received low prices for their produce. Under the Agricultural Adjustment Act (AAA), farmers were paid not to grow crops, thereby cutting production and forcing prices up. One of the most ambitious projects was the Tennessee Valley Authority (TVA). The area drained by the Tennessee River and its tributaries spanned seven states. Constant severe flooding washed the soil away and made it impossible for farmers to plant crops. The TVA employed men to build 21 dams to stop the flooding. The lakes behind the dams were used to make cheap **hydro-electricity** for farms and factories.

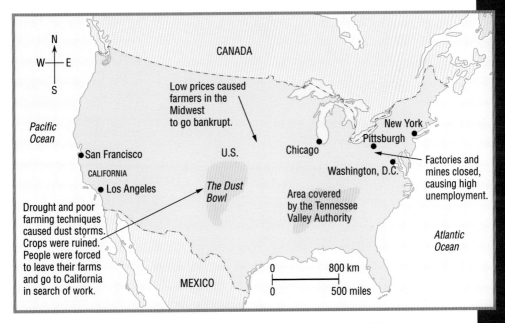

▲ This map shows the U.S. during the Great Depression of the 1930s.

The American people were grateful to Roosevelt and came to look upon him as a personal friend. Each day Roosevelt received between 5,000 and 8,000 letters, thanking him for his help. The president cleverly gave the pretense that he read and answered each letter himself. In fact, he employed extra staff to reply to the letters, allowing them to sign his name.

## Thanks, Mr. President

*Dear Mr. President*
*This is just to let you know that everything is all right now. The man you sent found our house all right, and we went down to the bank with him and the mortgage can go on for a while longer. You remember I wrote you about losing the furniture too. Well, your man got it back for us. I never heard of a president like you.*

*[Mr. President]*
*If you visit Dallas I will fix you a real dinner of hot biscuits, fried potatoes, chicken, chicken gravy, and butterscotch pie. We have a comfortable home, something that a working man could not have had prior to your presidency.*

(Examples of letters written to Roosevelt in the mid-1930s)

## Daily routine at the White House

Each morning Roosevelt ate his breakfast in his bedroom while he worked on government reports and read the newspapers. At about 10:30 A.M., he went to his office using a small wheelchair. He then met a large number of visitors who wished to discuss a variety of topics with him. Roosevelt enjoyed meeting people, and they generally felt very relaxed in his company. He took his lunch at his desk and spent the afternoon working. He left his office at 5:30 P.M. and went swimming in the White House pool. Sometimes he would conduct a conversation with an aide while he was swimming. He had dinner at 9:00 P.M. Even at the busiest times, Roosevelt still found time for his hobbies. He loved to play poker, read novels, keep his stamp collection up to date, and attend baseball games. Roosevelt read so quickly that a 700-page novel took him just an evening to read.

## Eleanor's role in the New Deal

During this period, Eleanor Roosevelt became the "eyes and ears" of the president. She was more mobile and able to travel to places her husband could not. She visited factories, farms, city slums, and coal mines across the U.S. She then reported her observations to her husband, often recommending what line of action he should take. Eleanor also wrote her own newspaper column, entitled "My Day," and campaigned hard for **civil rights** for African Americans in the southern states, and equal rights for women. In addition, she found time to help charities raise funds and to give speeches on issues close to her heart. She came to be respected and admired by millions of Americans.

▶ *Eleanor Roosevelt spoke at the "Century of Progress" exhibition in Chicago in 1933.*

# 7 The Second New Deal

In 1935, Roosevelt introduced a series of measures that became known as the second New Deal. With 11 million people still unemployed, the Works Progress Administration (WPA) was set up to create jobs. Under the leadership of Harry L. Hopkins (see page 58), the WPA provided work for over 8 million people between 1935 and 1943. The WPA paid workers an average of $55 a month to build roads, airports, hospitals, schools, and playgrounds. It also provided work for writers, artists, actors, and photographers. By 1937, unemployment had fallen to 8 million, the lowest since 1931.

▼ *WPA workers are shown here repairing a road in Louisville, Kentucky.*

## Social justice

Roosevelt wanted more social justice in the U.S. He believed that people deserved decent wages and working conditions, and that the country's wealth should be more evenly distributed. In July 1935, **Congress** passed the Wagner Act, which gave workers the right to organize **trade unions** and negotiate improved working conditions with their employers. This was followed in August by the Social Security Act, which was largely the work of Frances Perkins, the secretary of labor and the first woman to serve in a presidential **cabinet.** The act provided pensions for people over age 65 and paid unemployment insurance to people who had lost their jobs. To fund these measures, Roosevelt imposed higher taxes on companies and wealthier people.

## Opponents of the New Deal

Not all Americans supported the New Deal. Roosevelt's critics said he was "soaking the successful" and that the New Deal should be renamed the "Raw Deal." In some households, the word *Roosevelt* was banned and the president was simply referred to as "that man." Many **Republicans** said the **federal government** was interfering too much with business and the lives of ordinary people. Too much money was being wasted, taxes were too high, and Roosevelt was a **"dictator."**

Others, however, said that Roosevelt had not done enough to help the poor and jobless. Huey "Kingfish" Long, the governor of Louisiana, set up the Share Our Wealth Society, which called for old age pensions and a national minimum wage. Long argued that money should be taken from the rich and given to the poor so that every family had an income of at least $2,000 a year. He attracted a lot of support and planned to stand against Roosevelt in the 1936 presidential election.

However, Long was assassinated by a political opponent in 1935. Dr. Francis Townsend, a doctor from Long Beach, California, who campaigned on behalf of older people, said that people should have a pension of $200 per month after the age of 60. Another outspoken critic of the New Deal was Father Charles Coughlin, the "radio priest." He formed the National Union for Social Justice to campaign for higher wages. Coughlin's radio program regularly attracted audiences of up to 40 million people.

FOR A SUMMARY OF THE U.S. SYSTEM OF GOVERNMENT, SEE PAGE 59.

In 1935–1936, Roosevelt came into conflict with the **Supreme Court.** The court ruled that the NRA and the Agricultural Adjustment Act were not in line with the **Constitution** and were therefore illegal. It said that industry and agriculture were the business of each individual state and the federal government had no right to interfere. Roosevelt was angry at the court's decision and was worried that it might also declare the TVA, the Wagner Act, and the Social Security Act illegal.

## The 1936 presidential election

Although the New Deal had not ended the **Great Depression,** the lives of many ordinary Americans had improved since 1932. During the presidential election campaign of 1936, enthusiastic crowds greeted Roosevelt wherever he went. His Republican opponent, Alfred M. Landon, the governor of Kansas, criticized the New Deal, saying it had interfered with individual freedom. Roosevelt, however, had a landslide victory, carrying 46 out of 48 states and receiving 61 percent of the popular vote. "Everyone is against the New Deal except the voter," quipped the president. In his second **Inauguration Day** speech, Roosevelt told the crowd that he intended to "paint out" injustice in the country. It was a clear message that he believed more had to be done to create a fairer society.

## No match for FDR

*"If Landon had made one more speech, Roosevelt would have carried Canada!"*

Dorothy Thompson, a magazine columnist, was not impressed with Alfred Landon's campaigning skills in the 1936 election. Roosevelt was so popular with the voters that Landon stood little chance of winning.

## Problems and criticism

In early 1937, Roosevelt made a forlorn attempt to change the structure of the Supreme Court. He wanted to stop it from wrecking any more New Deal measures. Roosevelt proposed increasing the number of judges from nine to fifteen. The proposal caused an uproar. Roosevelt's critics said he was trying to "pack" the court with judges who supported the New Deal. Congress voted against the proposal. Roosevelt had made one of his biggest mistakes, and his image was tarnished. He even lost the support of some **Democratic** politicians over the issue. As it turned out, the Supreme Court later changed its attitude to the New Deal and did not oppose any more legislation.

▶ This cartoon comments on the controversy caused by Roosevelt's attempt to "pack" the Supreme Court with judges.

▲ *Violence flared between strikers and police at the Republic Steel Works in south Chicago in 1937.*

Roosevelt had an unhappy time during 1937 and 1938. As a result of the Wagner Act, there was an increase in trade union membership in 1937. Many employers, including Henry Ford (see page 58), did not like this and tried to break up the unions. There were a number of strikes, some of which resulted in violence. The worst incident occurred in Chicago on Memorial Day, May 31, 1937, when strikers at the Republic Steel Works clashed with police. Ten people were killed and eighty-four were injured.

There was also a drop in world trade in 1937. The demand for industrial goods fell in the U.S., and factories trimmed back their workforces. Unemployment rose from 8 to 10 million, and those with work had their wages cut. People blamed the president and called it the "Roosevelt recession." Things began to improve in 1938, but even so, the Republicans won a majority of seats in Congress in the November elections of that year. After this, the New Deal came to a halt.

## The New Deal: success or failure?

The New Deal got industry moving for a time, and the TVA was successful in making the Tennessee Valley a prosperous region. Relief programs provided the jobless with work, shelter, clothing, and food. Many looked up to Roosevelt and were inspired by his optimism and cheerfulness. They were comforted by the fact that the federal government now seemed willing to help people attain a reasonable standard of living. For the first time ever, old age pensions and unemployment pay were available to American citizens.

On the down side, the New Deal did very little for African Americans as a distinct group. African Americans were no nearer achieving **civil rights** and, despite the efforts of Eleanor Roosevelt, women did not achieve equality with men. By 1939, the New Deal had not stamped out poverty in the U.S. An estimated one-third of the population was still inadequately clothed and fed, and 9 million people were out of work. It took the outbreak of World War II to fully end the **Great Depression** in the U.S.

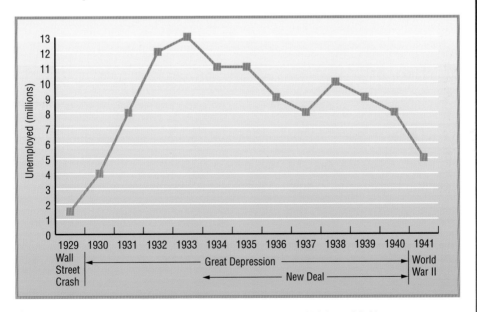

▲ *This chart tracks unemployment in the U.S. from 1929 to 1941.*

# 8 From Isolation to War

FOR DETAILS ON KEY PEOPLE OF ROOSEVELT'S TIME, SEE PAGE 58.

Since the end of **World War I** in 1918, the U.S. had followed a policy of **isolationism** and mainly kept out of international affairs. Roosevelt continued this policy when he first became president in 1933, although he did introduce the "good neighbor policy" to encourage friendly relations with Latin America. In 1935 and 1937, **Congress** passed two neutrality laws that underlined the determination of the U.S. to not get involved in any foreign wars.

Trouble, however, was brewing in Europe. Both Germany and Italy were under the control of aggressive **fascist dictators.** In 1935, Benito Mussolini, the Italian dictator, ordered an unprovoked invasion of Abyssinia, and in 1938, Adolf Hitler, the leader of **Nazi Germany,** occupied Austria and part of what was then Czechoslovakia. At first, Great Britain and France did nothing to stop these acts of aggression. Events then spiraled out of control, and by September 1939, Britain and France were at war with Germany.

## Key dates: buildup to World War II

| | | |
|---|---|---|
| **1934** | Hitler becomes dictator of Germany. | |
| **1938** | • March | Germany occupies Austria. |
| | • September | Germany invades the Sudetenland, part of Czechoslovakia. Hitler promises that he will take no more territory. |
| **1939** | • March | Germany invades the rest of Czechoslovakia. |
| | • September 1 | Germany invades Poland. |
| | • September 3 | Britain and France finally decide that Hitler has to be stopped, and declare war on Germany. World War II starts. |

## FDR's third term

Most Americans thought that the U.S. should stay out of the war in Europe. Roosevelt announced that the U.S. would stay neutral. But by November 1939, he had decided to help Britain. He asked Congress to **repeal** the neutrality laws to enable the British to buy American weapons. In June 1940, with the fall of France and with most of western Europe occupied by Germany, Roosevelt decided to stand for a third term of office. His **Republican** opponent was Wendell Wilkie, a businessman from Indiana and a fierce critic of the New Deal. After an exhausting campaign, Roosevelt defeated Wilkie by nearly 5 million votes. It was clear that the American people still had confidence in Roosevelt and believed that he had the necessary experience to lead them through another difficult period.

After the election, a tired Roosevelt went on a cruise in the Caribbean Ocean. He was still battling against his disability. Every movement he made took a huge amount of effort. Although he was able to lift himself out of his wheelchair, he still had to be carried upstairs and helped in and out of motor cars. However, the president spent several days playing poker and deep-sea fishing before returning to the White House refreshed.

▶ *German troops marched into Paris, the French capital, on June 14, 1940. By this time most of western Europe was under German control.*

By the end of 1940, Britain was on the verge of bankruptcy. The British prime minister, Winston Churchill (see page 58), informed Roosevelt that Britain could no longer afford to buy American equipment and appealed for help. Roosevelt decided that the U.S. would lend Britain equipment and goods. When he announced this proposal, isolationists demonstrated in Washington, D.C., and New York. But Roosevelt argued his case well, and in March 1941, Congress passed the **Lend-Lease Act.** By 1945, the U.S. had provided $50 billion worth of equipment to the **Allies.**

In August 1941, Roosevelt met Churchill on board the U.S.S. *Augusta* off the Newfoundland coast. The two men struck up an instant friendship and signed the Atlantic Charter, a document which stated that "after the war all men shall be enabled to live in freedom from want and fear." This principle later formed the basis for the founding of the **United Nations** in 1945. In September, German submarines attacked American shipping in the Atlantic. Roosevelt, however, held back from asking Congress to declare war.

Roosevelt suffered a personal blow when his mother, Sara, died in early September 1941 at the age of 85. Sara had been ill since the summer and Roosevelt had visited her just three days before her death. She had appeared to be in good spirits and her sudden death came as a great shock to him.

## Pearl Harbor

At the same time, events in Asia were worrying the president. Japan had already occupied China and French Indo-China, now known as Cambodia, Laos, and Vietnam. Clearly, the Japanese were intent on building an **empire** in Asia and the Pacific.

Roosevelt tried to organize talks with the Japanese to stabilize the situation, but no progress was made. Then, on the morning of Sunday, December 7, 1941, the Japanese launched a surprise attack on the American naval base at **Pearl Harbor** in Hawaii. The following day, a serious-looking Roosevelt spoke to Congress and asked for a state of war to be declared against Japan. Helped to the podium by his son, James, the president told Congress that December 7, 1941, was "a date which will live in infamy." Just 33 minutes after he had completed his speech, Congress voted overwhelmingly to declare war on Japan. The question as to whether the U.S. should get involved directly in World War II had been answered for the president by Japanese aggression. Germany, in support of its Japanese ally, declared war on the U.S. Isolationists now joined other Americans to stand behind Roosevelt.

**Pearl Harbor fact file**

American losses:

- 18 naval vessels either sunk or damaged
- 265 aircraft destroyed
- 2,403 killed
- 1,178 injured

▼ *The U.S. destroyer* Shaw *is shown here on fire in Pearl Harbor after being hit by Japanese bombs.*

37

Things looked bleak for the U.S. and its **Allies** at the start of 1942. The Japanese were on the rampage in the Pacific. They had already captured the American islands of Guam and Wake and had invaded the Philippines. In Europe, the Germans were advancing deep into the **Soviet Union,** and they had the British on the retreat in North Africa.

Roosevelt realized that he had to lift the morale of the American nation and, on February 23, 1942, the 210th anniversary of the birth of George Washington, he gave one of his most impressive radio "fireside chats." Beforehand, Roosevelt had requested that people have a map of the world available to refer to as he spoke. He then explained simply what was happening in each part of the world where the war was being fought, before ending with a rallying call to lift spirits. It was a masterful performance.

In the weeks that followed, Roosevelt toured the U.S. visiting naval bases, army camps, and weapons factories. Eleanor was also heavily involved in the war effort, visiting wounded American soldiers in military hospitals across the world.

### Roosevelt's rallying call

*"From Berlin, Rome, and Tokyo we have been described as a nation of weaklings.*
*Let them repeat that now!*
*Let them tell that to General MacArthur and his men.*
*Let them tell that to the sailors who today are hitting hard in the far waters of the Pacific.*
*Let them tell that to the boys in the* Flying Fortresses.
*Let them tell that to the Marines!"*

(From Roosevelt's "fireside chat," February 23, 1942)

## Military planning

Roosevelt gathered a group of top military advisers around him to discuss military strategy. After a great deal of argument, they decided to concentrate first on defeating the Germans and Italians in Europe and North Africa. This was a controversial decision, as most Americans, still angry about the attack on **Pearl Harbor,** wanted to see Japan beaten before anyone else. Roosevelt, however, stuck to his decision. Throughout the war, the president's leadership style was to initiate and make the big decisions but, once made, he left the battle details to his generals.

Many of his closest advisers were amazed at how relaxed Roosevelt appeared to be. One observed that he only spent half the week on war matters and always managed to keep his stamp collection up to date!

▲ *Roosevelt is shown here on a visit to a Flying Fortress aircraft factory in Long Beach, California, in 1942.*

In the summer of 1942, the fortunes of the Allies began to improve. In the Pacific, the Americans defeated the Japanese in the **Battles of the Coral Sea** in May and **Midway Island** in June. Then, in October, the British routed the Germans in the **Battle of El Alamein** in North Africa.

## Roosevelt and Churchill

In January 1943, Roosevelt met Churchill in Casablanca in Morocco, Africa, to plan the next Allied attacks in the war. Joseph Stalin (see page 58), the Soviet leader, refused to attend the meeting, as the **Red Army** was fighting against the Germans at the crucial **Battle of Stalingrad.** To get to Casablanca, Roosevelt had to make a dangerous journey of 7,000 miles (11,200 kilometers) by rail, sea, and air. He was the first American president to fly in an airplane, and many of his advisers were nervous about the trip, fearing the enemy would shoot them down. A number of them suffered acute air sickness as they flew over the Atlantic Ocean. Roosevelt, however, enjoyed every minute of the exhausting journey and arrived in Casablanca looking remarkably fresh. At the conclusion of the conference, Roosevelt and Churchill announced that the Allies would invade Sicily and then launch an invasion of northern France "sometime in 1944." They also said that the Allies would fight until the **Axis powers** accepted an unconditional surrender.

The two leaders got along well. They exchanged hundreds of messages and frequently spoke on the telephone. Altogether, they had nine face-to-face meetings, with Churchill staying either in the White House or at the Roosevelt estate in Hyde Park. Roosevelt enjoyed driving the British prime minister around his estate in his hand-controlled motor car. The two men felt at ease in each other's company, and Churchill said he had the "utmost confidence" in the American president.

## The turn of the tide

During 1943, the war turned in favor of the Allies. At the end
of January, the Red Army won the Battle of Stalingrad and
began to push the Germans back toward Poland. In the
Pacific, helped by Australian forces, the Americans had
embarked on an "island-hopping" strategy that involved taking
Japanese bases one by one until they were within range of
Japan itself. In July, the Allies invaded Sicily and Italy, and by
September they had forced the Italians to surrender. At the
end of 1943, the "Big Three"—Roosevelt, Churchill, and
Stalin—met in Tehran in Persia, now known as Iran, where
they made preparations for the invasion of France in 1944.

▼ This map tracks the progression of World War II in Asia and the Pacific Ocean.

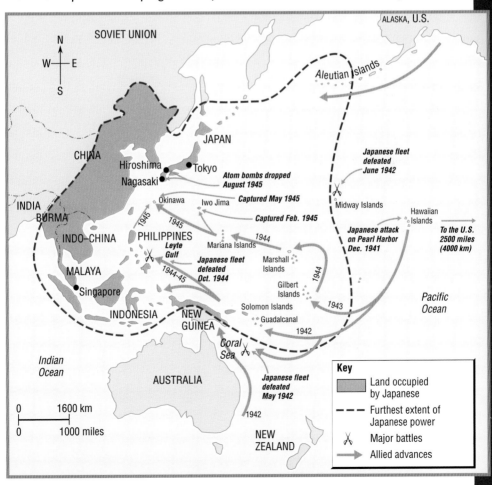

On his return to the U.S. from Tehran, Roosevelt complained of headaches and flu symptoms. He was very tired and fell asleep at his desk on several occasions. By January 1944, he had made little improvement and began visiting Hyde Park each weekend in an effort to regain his health. In March, he went for a check-up at the Bethesda Naval Hospital in Maryland, Virginia. The doctors found that his arteries were closing up and that he was in danger of suffering a heart attack. Roosevelt was ordered to get more rest and cut down on his smoking, but the American public was not informed of his condition. People close to him, however, could not help but notice the bags under his eyes, his grey complexion, and his failing memory.

## D-Day

On June 6, 1944, over 150,000 Allied troops, under the leadership of General Eisenhower (see page 58), landed on the beaches of Normandy in northern France. From there they began to push the German army back toward Berlin. In eastern Europe, Soviet troops had advanced into German-occupied Poland, Romania, and Bulgaria. It was only a matter of time before the Germans were defeated. In the Pacific, the Americans had inflicted a crushing defeat on the Japanese in the Philippines.

◀ *This photograph shows American troops wading ashore onto the beaches of Normandy on D-Day, June 6, 1944.*

## The post-war world

Roosevelt said that after the war a new peace-keeping organization known as the **United Nations** should be set up. He made it clear that in the future, the U.S. should play a leading role in international affairs and abandon the policy of **isolationism.** There was some concern, however, about the **communist** Soviet Union. Would Stalin hold onto the countries that the Soviets had liberated from German occupation and install communist governments? Roosevelt was confident that Stalin was not trying to take over eastern Europe, but this issue was to come to the forefront when the "Big Three" met at Yalta in February 1945.

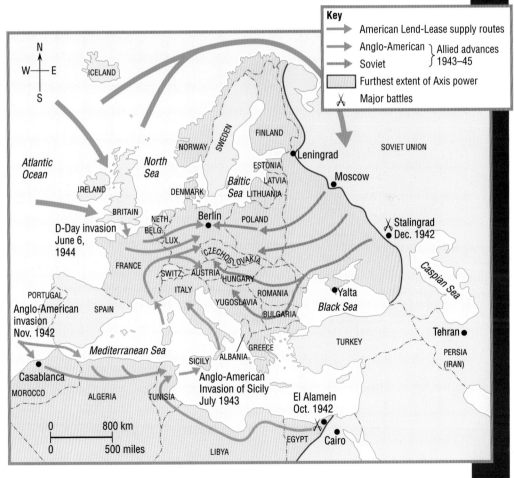

▲ This map tracks the progression of World War II in Europe and North Africa.

# 10 The Home Front

At home, the war brought an end to unemployment. Roosevelt set up a number of agencies, such as the War Production Board, to mobilize the workforce to manufacture weapons, ships, tanks, and aircraft. Each war industry was given a production target. Many factory owners complained that the targets were far too high, but Roosevelt brushed aside their complaints, saying, "Oh . . . the production people can do it if they really try!" The president also sanctioned the "Manhattan Project" to develop an atomic bomb. Despite the rationing of food, rubber, and fuel, most Americans enjoyed a much better standard of living than they had in the 1930s. Wages were generally high, and there was plenty of work to be had.

## Home front fact file

Average time to build a warship:
- 1940: 355 days
- 1943: 56 days

Unemployment:
- 1940: 14.6 million
- 1944: 1.2 million

Average individual income:
- 1939: $691 per year
- 1945: $1,515 per year

## Problems for the president

Many liberal politicians hoped that Roosevelt would introduce more New Deal legislation. But his mind was now focused on winning the war and, as unemployment was low, he allowed **Congress** to abolish a number of New Deal agencies, such as the Works Progress Administration.

Relations between the **trade unions** and employers were generally good during the war. But in 1943, the miners and steelworkers held a series of strikes, demanding higher wages. Although the disputes were settled, Roosevelt asked Congress to pass a national service law so that all adults could be directed to work in war industries if required. Congress, however, refused to cooperate. From about 1943 onward, the president had a distinctly cool relationship with Congress.

Race relations was also a problem. During the war, African Americans were treated unfairly in the workplace. They were given menial jobs and paid less than their white counterparts. In the armed services, there were separate units for African Americans and whites, and many generals believed African Americans were incapable of holding top positions. Roosevelt hated racism but, despite Eleanor's urging, did little to give African Americans equal rights. He was too frightened that he would lose the votes of whites in the South. African Americans, however, showed they were worthy of better treatment with their patriotism in the war effort and by calling for "Double V"—victory in the war and victory against racism at home.

Roosevelt's treatment of Americans of Japanese descent was a stain on his wartime record at home. It was feared that they would send secret information to Japan, so in 1942, Roosevelt ordered 120,000 Japanese Americans to be detained in special camps. Despite this, over 17,000 Japanese Americans fought heroically on the **Allied** side during the war.

▶ By 1944, a third of the workers in American industry were women. "Rosie the Riveter," shown here, was a cartoon character used to entice women into war industries.

### The 1944 presidential campaign

In July 1944, with his health failing rapidly, Roosevelt accepted the **Democratic** Party nomination to run for a fourth term of office. Harry S. Truman, a Missouri senator, was selected to run for vice president. Roosevelt was up against Thomas E. Dewey, the **Republican** governor of New York. There was little difference between the two men's policies and Dewey resorted to making Roosevelt's poor health an election issue. The majority of Americans, however, still held Roosevelt in high esteem and crowds flocked to see him when he appeared in public. On October 21, 1944, a cold and wet Saturday, Roosevelt was driven for four hours through the streets of New York in an open-topped car. Thousands of New Yorkers cheered and clapped and, according to Eleanor, the president found it an "exhilarating" experience. Roosevelt's campaign was also boosted by a one-hour radio program paid for by the Democratic Party. It consisted of a series of jokes poking fun at Dewey. Many Hollywood film stars, such as Judy Garland

For a summary of the U.S. system of government, see page 59.

### Faithful companion

Roosevelt's Scottish terrier dog, Fala, was given to him by Margaret Suckley, a distant cousin. Fala went everywhere with the president, even sleeping in his room at night. During the 1944 election campaign, the Republicans put out a false story that Roosevelt had left Fala behind in the Aleutian Islands after a recent visit. They went on to claim that a warship had been sent to collect the dog, at an enormous cost to the taxpayer. Roosevelt turned the tables by using the story to ridicule the Republicans, saying that he didn't mind being unfairly attacked but Fala had been most upset.

46

and Groucho Marx, also came on the program to express their support for Roosevelt. Roosevelt won the election, claiming 53.5 percent of the popular vote to Dewey's 46 percent.

Soon afterward, on November 27, 1944, Roosevelt went to Warm Springs to rest. Stress was taking its toll, and his blood pressure was alarmingly high. Roosevelt spent three weeks reading, swimming in the pool, and driving around the grounds. He felt refreshed when he returned to Washington, D.C., in time for **Inauguration Day** on January 20, 1945.

▲ *This photograph was taken on Inauguration Day, January 20, 1945. Franklin and Eleanor Roosevelt were photographed in the White House with their thirteen grandchildren.*

# 11 The Final Months

On January 23, 1945, Roosevelt set sail on the first stage of an arduous journey to meet Churchill and Stalin at Yalta in the Crimea. After a brief stopover in Malta, the president completed the trip by air. The Yalta conference opened on February 4, by which time Germany was on the brink of defeat. British and American forces were closing in on the River Rhine, and Soviet troops were in occupation of large amounts of territory in eastern Europe. The three leaders discussed the future of Germany and eastern Europe, and the war against Japan.

## The Yalta agreements

After eight days of intensive talks, the "Big Three" announced what they had decided about the post-war world:

- The **United Nations** organization would be set up in April 1945.
- The **Soviet Union** would enter the war against Japan after Germany had finally been defeated. (This in fact did not happen.)
- Germany was to be divided into four zones of **Allied** occupation, one each to be run by the U.S., the Soviet Union, Great Britain, and France.

◀ The "Big Three" posed for the cameras at Yalta. They are, from left to right, Churchill, Roosevelt, and Stalin.

- Leaders from **Nazi Germany** would be put on trial for **war crimes.**
- Stalin promised that countries in eastern Europe, then occupied by the **Red Army,** could hold **free elections** to choose their governments.

On his return to Washington, Roosevelt addressed **Congress** on March 1, 1945. He looked frail and tired. Senators and congressmen who had not seen him for a while were taken aback by the way he looked, and many were convinced that they would not see him alive again. For the first time ever, the president entered the chamber in a wheelchair and made his speech sitting down. He started by saying:

"I hope that you will pardon me for an unusual posture of sitting down . . . but I know that you will realize that it makes it a lot easier for me in not having to carry about ten pounds of steel around on the bottom of my legs; and also because I have just completed a 14,000 mile [22,400 kilometer] trip."

The rest of his speech conveyed a message of optimism and hope for the future. In a faltering voice, the president said he was confident that the U.S., the Soviet Union, and Britain would work well together after the war to maintain the peace. He also told Congress that he was looking forward to a meeting in San Francisco on April 25, where the **United Nations Charter** would be drawn up.

Roosevelt was desperately in need of a rest, but felt he could be "in trim again" if he went to Warm Springs health spa for a few days. Accompanied by his cousins, Margaret Suckley and Laura Delano, he arrived there on March 30, 1945. He slept in each day, before going through his mail and reading the newspapers.

The sun put some color back into Roosevelt's cheeks and he appeared to be regaining his strength. Feeling more relaxed, he was able to go for drives through the countryside.

At midday on Thursday, April 12, Elizabeth Shoumatoff arrived to continue the portrait she was painting of the president. At about 1:15 P.M., as he was sitting for the artist, Roosevelt complained of a "terrific headache" and slouched forward in his chair. His two doctors were immediately called. The president had suffered a brain hemorrhage. He was taken to his bedroom unconscious and, despite being given artificial respiration, was pronounced dead at 3:35 P.M. He was 63 years old. Eleanor Roosevelt was informed of her husband's death by telephone in New York. In a message to her four sons, away with the armed services, Eleanor said, "He slept away this afternoon. He did his job to the end as he would have wanted." Americans everywhere were in a state of profound shock at the passing of "their friend."

## The last journey home
Roosevelt's body was taken by train to Washington, D.C. People lined the route in a somber mood to pay their last respects. They were stunned by the president's death. In Washington, thousands more watched as the funeral procession made its way from Union Station to the White House, where a short service was held. On the evening of April 14, the funeral train of seventeen carriages left Washington bound for Hyde Park. Sitting in one of the carriages were Eleanor, the rest of the family, except three sons who were abroad, Harry S. Truman, who was now president, and Fala the dog. On April 15, a cold Sunday morning, Roosevelt was laid to rest in the rose garden at Springwood.

## Key dates: the end of World War II

**1945**
- April 30      Hitler commits suicide.
- May 8      Germany surrenders.
- August 6      President Truman, who had succeeded Roosevelt, orders the dropping of an atomic bomb on Hiroshima in Japan.
- August 9      A second atomic bomb is dropped, on Nagasaki.
- August 14      Japan surrenders.

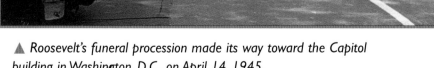

▲ Roosevelt's funeral procession made its way toward the Capitol building in Washington, D.C., on April 14, 1945.

In his twelve years as president, Franklin Roosevelt successfully led the U.S. through the **Great Depression** and World War II, two of the most catastrophic episodes in the history of the twentieth century. In doing this, he left a powerful legacy for future generations.

## The New Deal

One of Roosevelt's most important legacies was that he changed the way the American people viewed the role of the **federal government.** Before his presidency, it was widely thought that the federal government should stay out of the economy and the lives of individuals. The New Deal, however, involved the federal government playing a central role in shaping people's lives. Since then, people in the U.S. have come to accept the idea that the central government has a duty to look after its citizens and intervene in the economy at difficult times. Some New Deal measures, such as social security and unemployment pay, are still integral to American society and those of other democratic countries. The U.S. **stock market** is still regulated by the Securities and Exchange Commission, a federal government agency introduced by Roosevelt in 1934 with the aim of preventing another Wall Street crash. The Tennessee Valley Authority, set up in 1933, is still providing cheap electricity for 8 million people and managing flood control, land use, and recreation. No wonder people say, "It's a Deal that keeps going."

Roosevelt's charisma was such that he made the presidency more influential than both the **Congress** and the **Supreme Court.** The presidents who followed him had more authority and prestige than ever before.

## International affairs

Roosevelt convinced Americans that the U.S. had a responsibility to be a world leader, defending democracy and human rights. No longer could the U.S. operate a policy of **isolationism** as it had done between 1919 and 1941. This led Roosevelt, in the face of opposition from many Americans, to support Britain and France in the early months of World War II. He was also instrumental in the establishment of the **United Nations** to uphold world peace. Unfortunately, he died before the UN officially came into existence. His influence, however, is enshrined in the **United Nations Charter,** which is based on his "four freedoms" of basic human rights (see box below), first declared in a speech to Congress on January 6, 1941.

### Roosevelt's four freedoms

*"We look forward to a world founded upon . . . freedom of speech, freedom of every person to worship God in his own way, freedom from want, and freedom from fear."*

(Roosevelt to Congress, January 6, 1941)

▶ *This American poster from 1943 vividly depicts Roosevelt's "four freedoms."*

OURS...to fight for

*Freedom of Speech*

*Freedom of Worship*

*Freedom from Want*

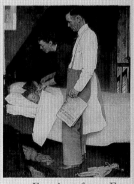
*Freedom from Fear*

Roosevelt's wife, Eleanor, went on to make a vital contribution to the early work of the United Nations. At the request of President Truman, she served on the U.S. delegation to the first meeting of the United Nations General Assembly in London in January 1946. She later became the chairperson of a UN commission that was set up to devise a Declaration of Human Rights for the world. The commission was successful in its work and the Declaration of Human Rights was formally adopted by the world's nations on December 10, 1948. Eleanor remained politically active until her death from tuberculosis in November 1962, at the age of 78.

## Unfair criticism?

A major feature of the post-war world turned out to be the Cold War, which lasted from 1945 to 1989. This was a period of mutual distrust and suspicion between the U.S. and its **Allies** and the **Soviet Union.** Roosevelt's critics have blamed him for this situation, saying he should have been tougher with Stalin at Yalta. He should have made Stalin hold **free elections** in eastern Europe, rather than taking his promises at face value. As it turned out, no free elections ever took place in eastern Europe. Instead, between 1945 and 1948, **communist** governments loyal to Moscow were set up in Poland, Hungary, Romania, Bulgaria, and Czechoslovakia. The **Western powers** felt cheated, and this made them wary of the Soviet Union. Roosevelt, however, did what he thought was right at Yalta. To blame him for the Cold War seems unreasonable.

## The March of Dimes

As well as developing a treatment center for **polio** sufferers at Warm Springs, Roosevelt helped to set up the National Foundation for Infantile Paralysis in 1934 to raise money for research into polio. By 1938, the organization had become known as the "March of Dimes," because most people were poor during the Depression and could only afford to donate dimes or other small coins toward the cause. Nonetheless, it raised millions of dollars to fund research, resulting in the development of the first polio **vaccine** in 1954. Since then, polio has virtually been wiped out in countries where vaccine programs have been effectively introduced. Roosevelt has been called a "disabled hero" because his paralysis did not prevent him from becoming one of the greatest American presidents. He showed that physical disability was not a barrier to achievement in life, setting an example for disabled people throughout the world.

On a visit to Warm Springs in 1995, President Bill Clinton summed up Roosevelt's achievements with these words: "He showed us how to be a nation in times of great stress . . . He taught us about the human spirit . . . He led us from the depths of economic despair, through a depression to victory in the war, to the threshold of the promise of the post-war America he unfortunately never lived to see. He did all these things and so many more to change America and the world."

▶ *This Franklin D. Roosevelt Memorial statue stands in Washington, D.C.*

# Timeline

**1882** Franklin is born at Springwood, Hyde Park, New York, January 30.

**1896** Franklin is sent to Groton Preparatory School in Massachusetts.

**1900** Franklin attends Harvard University.

**1904** Roosevelt enters Columbia Law School in New York.

**1905** Franklin marries Anna Eleanor Roosevelt on March 17.

**1906** Their first child, Anna Eleanor, is born.

**1907** Roosevelt starts work as a junior clerk in a New York law firm.
His second child, James, is born.

**1909** Roosevelt's third child, Franklin Jr., is born in March, but dies in November.

**1910** Roosevelt wins election to the New York state senate.
His fourth child, Elliott, is born.

**1912** Roosevelt is reelected to the New York state senate.

**1913** Roosevelt is appointed assistant secretary to the U.S. Navy by President Woodrow Wilson.

**1914** **World War I** begins.
Roosevelt's fifth child, Franklin Jr., is born.

**1916** Roosevelt's sixth and last child, John, is born.

**1917** The U.S. enters World War I in April. Roosevelt organizes the Navy.

**1920** Roosevelt resigns from the Navy and runs for vice president alongside the **Democratic** Party's presidential candidate, James N. Cox. They lose to the **Republican** candidate, Warren G. Harding.

**1921** Roosevelt is struck down by **polio** and is left paralyzed from the waist down.

**1922** Roosevelt speaks at the Democratic Party **Convention** in New York.

**1927** Roosevelt establishes Warm Springs, Georgia, as a treatment center for polio victims.

**1928** Roosevelt becomes the governor of New York.

**1929** The Wall Street crash in October plunges the U.S. and the rest of the world into the **Great Depression.**

**1930** Roosevelt is reelected governor of New York.

**1932** Roosevelt is elected the 32nd president of the U.S. and pledges a "New Deal" for the American people.

**1933** Roosevelt gives the first of his "fireside chats" on March 12. During the 100 days from March 9 to June 16, many new measures, such as the Civilian Conservation Corps, are introduced under the first New Deal.

**1933** The Tennessee Valley Authority is established. Adolf Hitler is appointed the chancellor (president) of Germany.

**1934** Hitler declares himself the Führer **(dictator)** of Germany.

**1935** The Wagner Act and Social Security Act form the basis of the second New Deal.

**1935** The **Supreme Court** declares the National Recovery Administration and the Agricultural Adjustment Act illegal.

**1936** Roosevelt is reelected president for a second term of office.

**1937** Roosevelt fails to "pack" the Supreme Court by appointing six more judges. The "Roosevelt Recession" starts in September and goes on until June 1938.

**1938** Hitler occupies Austria in March and invades the Sudetenland in September.

**1939** Hitler invades Poland on September 1. Britain and France declare war on Germany on September 3. World War II begins.

**1940** During April, May, and June, German forces overrun Denmark, Norway, the Netherlands, Belgium, Luxembourg, and France. Roosevelt is reelected president in November.

**1941** Roosevelt signs the **Lend-Lease Act** on March 11. Roosevelt meets Winston Churchill, the British prime minister, off the coast of Newfoundland and signs the Atlantic Charter on August 9–12. Roosevelt's mother Sara dies on September 7. The Japanese attack **Pearl Harbor** on December 7. The U.S. declares war on Japan on December 8. Germany declares war on the U.S. on December 11.

**1942** British forces defeat the Germans at El Alamein in October. U.S. forces land in northern Africa in November.

**1943** Roosevelt and Churchill meet at the Casablanca Conference January 14–21. The "Big Three" (Roosevelt, Churchill, and Stalin) meet for the first time together at Tehran November 28–December 1.

**1944** The Anglo-American invasion of Normandy, France (D-Day), takes place June 6. Roosevelt is reelected for a fourth term of office.

**1945** The "Big Three" meet at Yalta February 4–12. Roosevelt dies of a brain hemorrhage on April 12 and is succeeded by Harry S. Truman. Germany surrenders May 8. Japan surrenders August 15, after atomic bombs are dropped on Hiroshima and Nagasaki.

**1962** Eleanor Roosevelt dies at age 78.

# Key People of Roosevelt's Time

*Churchill, Sir Winston* (1874–1965). Churchill was prime minister of Britain in 1940–1945 and 1951–1955. His inspirational speeches and determination guided Britain through the dark days of World War II.

*Eisenhower, General Dwight* (1890–1969). Eisenhower was appointed the supreme commander of the **Allied** forces in 1944. A **Republican** in politics, he became the 34th president of the United States of America, serving two terms in 1953–1961.

*Ford, Henry* (1863–1947). Ford founded the Ford Motor Company, which produced the Model T motor car between 1909 and 1926. Ford was strongly opposed to **trade unions.**

*Hitler, Adolf* (1889–1945). Hitler became chancellor (prime minister) of Germany in 1933 and proceeded to establish himself as Führer **(dictator)**. He was largely responsible for bringing about World War II and for the murder of 6 million Jewish people. He committed suicide in April 1945.

*Hopkins, Harry L.* (1890–1946). Hopkins was an adviser to Roosevelt and head of the Works Progress Administration (WPA) from 1935 through 1943. He accompanied Roosevelt on his trips to meet Churchill and Stalin during World War II.

*MacArthur, General Douglas* (1880–1964). MacArthur was supreme allied commander in the southwest Pacific from 1942. He played a big part in defeating Japan and formally accepted the Japanese surrender on board the U.S.S. *Missouri* on September 2, 1945.

*Mussolini, Benito* (1883–1945). Mussolini was the **fascist** dictator of Italy from 1922 through 1943, known as "*il Duce*" (the Leader). He took Italy into World War II, supporting Hitler. He was killed while trying to flee the country in 1945.

*Stalin, Joseph* (1878–1953). Stalin was dictator of the **Soviet Union** in 1927–1953. Stalin built up Soviet industry, but killed ("purged") 5 million Soviet people during the 1930s on the grounds that they were a threat to his rule.

*Wilson, Woodrow* (1856–1924). Wilson was a **Democrat** and the 28th president of the U.S. in 1913–1921. He took the U.S. into **World War I** in 1917. He was a strong advocate of the **League of Nations,** but failed to convince **Congress** that the U.S. should join.

# The U.S. System of Government

## Constitution

The United States is governed by its **Constitution,** a list of rules that were written down in 1787. Since then there have been 27 amendments, or changes, to the Constitution.

## Federal government

The **federal government** of the U.S. is based in Washington, D.C. It deals with matters that affect all 50 states, such as national taxes, foreign relations, welfare, and social security. The federal government is made up of three branches: executive, legislative, and judicial.

### Executive: President

The president is the head of the federal government and carries out the laws. The president is elected every four years. Due to a law passed in 1951, no president may serve more than two terms, or eight years, in office.

### Legislative: Congress

**Congress** is the law-making body of the federal government and consists of two houses: the House of Representatives and the Senate.

### Judicial: Supreme Court

This is the highest court in the land, with nine judges, each appointed by the president with the advice and consent of the Senate. The **Supreme Court** has the power to decide whether laws are unconstitutional.

*The House of Representatives:*
Made up of 435 congressmen and women, elected for two years.

*The Senate:*
Made up of 100 senators, two per state, elected for six years.

## State government

Each individual state has its own executive (governor), legislative (legislature), and judicial branches, based in the state's capital city. State governments deal with matters such as prisons, education, law and order, and local taxes.

# Sources for Further Research

Downing, David. *Benito Mussolini.* Chicago: Heinemann Library, 2001.

Downing, David. *The Great Depression.* Chicago: Heinemann Library, 2001.

Downing, David. *Joseph Stalin.* Chicago: Heinemann Library, 2001.

Isaacs, Sally Senzell. *America in the Time of Franklin Delano Roosevelt.* Chicago: Heinemann Library, 1999.

Joseph, Paul. *Franklin D. Roosevelt.* Edina, Minn.: ABDO Publishing Company, 2000.

Morris, Jeffrey B. *The FDR Way.* Minneapolis, Minn.: The Lerner Publishing Group, 1996.

Nardo, Don. *Franklin D. Roosevelt.* Broomall, Pa.: Chelsea House Publishers, 1996.

Polenberg, Richard. *The Era of Franklin D. Roosevelt, 1933–1945: A Brief History with Documents.* New York: Saint Martin's Press, 2000.

Reynoldson, Fiona. *Key Battles of World War II.* Chicago: Heinemann Library, 2001.

Reynoldson, Fiona. *Winston Churchill.* Chicago: Heinemann Library, 2001.

Schuman, Michael A. *Franklin D. Roosevelt: The Four-Term President.* Berkeley Heights, N.J.: Enslow Publishers, 1996.

Spies, Karen Bornemann. *Franklin D. Roosevelt.* Berkeley Heights, N.J.: Enslow Publishers, 1999.

Tames, Richard. *Pearl Harbor.* Chicago: Heinemann Library, 2001.

Taylor, David. *Adolf Hitler.* Chicago: Heinemann Library, 2001.

# Glossary

**Allies** the U.S., Great Britain, France, Australia, New Zealand, and the Soviet Union, who fought together against the Axis powers in World War II

**Axis powers** Germany, Italy, and Japan, who fought against the Allies during World War II

**cabinet** small group of politicians appointed by the president to help run the U.S.

**Campobello Island** island in the Bay of Fundy, off the coast of New Brunswick, Canada, where the Roosevelt family had a summer home

**civil rights** idea that all people, regardless of color or culture, should have equal rights in voting, education, employment, and housing

**communism** political system in which factories, mines, and farms are owned by the government and there is no private ownership. The Soviet Union became a communist country after the Russian Revolution of 1917.

**Congress** legislative branch of U.S. government, made up of the Senate and the House of Representatives

**Constitution** set of rules laying down how a country should be governed

**convention** political meeting or assembly

**Coral Sea, Battle of the** naval battle off the northeast coast of Australia in May 1942. The Japanese were forced back by Allied forces. Aircraft flying from aircraft carriers carried out the fighting.

**Democrat** person who supports or represents the Democratic Party, one of the two main political parties in the U.S. Democrats believe in federal government action to provide social welfare and to help industry and farming. Since the 1960s, they have advocated civil rights in the U.S.

**dictator** ruler with total authority in a country

**El Alamein, Battle of** crucial battle in Egypt from October 23 to November 4, 1942. The British Army, under General Bernard Montgomery, beat the German *Afrika Korps*, commanded by Erwin Rommel.

**empire** group of countries that are taken over and ruled by one powerful country

**fascist** system of government in which a dictator is in charge. The people cannot vote and are not allowed to criticize the leader.

**federal government** central government of the U.S., based in Washington, D.C., and headed by the president

**free elections** when people are able to vote in secret for the government of their choice

**governess** female teacher employed by well-off families to live with and educate their children at home

**Great Depression** period in the 1930s when there was a drop in world trade, following the Wall Street crash of 1929. The Depression brought unemployment and poverty to millions of people throughout the world.

**hydro-electricity** cheap electricity made by fast-flowing water driving turbines, which in turn power generators to produce electricity

**Inauguration Day** day the U.S. president is ceremonially admitted into office

**isolationism** U.S. policy of staying out of world affairs (pursued between 1918 and 1941)

**League of Nations** international peace-keeping organization set up in 1920 and disbanded in 1946

**Lend-Lease Act** Act of Congress signed by Roosevelt on March 11, 1941, that provided for the loan of war equipment to Britain and the Soviet Union

**Midway Island, Battle of** aircraft-carrier-based battle fought between the U.S. and Japan in the Pacific Ocean, June 3–6, 1942. It resulted in the first major defeat for the Japanese Navy.

**mortgage** loan made to people buying a house

**Nazi Germany** Germany under the control of Adolf Hitler and the Nazi Party between 1933 and 1945

**Pearl Harbor** American naval base in Hawaii, and scene of an unprovoked attack by the Japanese in December 1941

**polio** short for *poliomyelitis,* a disease resulting in paralysis

**Progressive era** period from the late 1890s to 1914, when many politicians believed that the federal government should tackle some of the social problems in the U.S., such as poor housing and working conditions

**Red Army** army of the Soviet Union from 1918 to 1991

**repeal** abolition of an Act of Congress

**Republican** person who supports or represents the Republican Party, one of the two main political parties in the U.S. Founded in 1854, it especially gets support from business and the higher income earners. Republicans believe that the federal government should play a minor role and that people should do things for themselves.

**shares** parts into which a company's stock are divided. People buy shares in companies and are paid a dividend out of the company's profits.

**soup kitchen** place that gives out free soup and other food to homeless and unemployed people

**Soviet Union** shortened name for the Union of Soviet Socialists Republics (USSR), formed in 1923 after the communists had seized control

**Stalingrad, Battle of** battle during which the city of Stalingrad was put under siege by the Germans in 1942–43. The Red Army counter-attacked and began to push the Germans back. It was a crucial turning point in World War II.

**stock market** place where shares are bought and sold— also called the stock exchange

**Supreme Court** highest court in the U.S., made up of nine judges appointed by the president. They decide if laws are in keeping with the U.S. Constitution.

**trade unions** groups that look after the welfare of workers in different trades. For example, trade unions bargain with the employers for improved working conditions.

**United Nations (UN)** international peace-keeping body of the world, set up in 1945, with its headquarters in New York

**United Nations Charter** document that lays down the aims and rules of the United Nations

**vaccine** substance, usually injected into the body, to prevent a person from catching a certain disease or virus

**war crimes** wartime crimes against humanity, such as mass murder of innocent civilians

**Western powers** after 1945, a phrase used to describe the U.S. and its allies in western Europe

**World War I** conflict between the Allies (Great Britain, France, Australia, New Zealand, and Russia) and the Central Powers (Germany, Austria-Hungary, and Turkey) in 1914–18. The U.S. entered the war in April 1917.

# Index